THE GOLD GUIDES

SORRENTO

AND THE AMALFI COAST

BAGNO DELLA REGINA GIOVANNA - MASSA LUBRENSE
SANT'AGATA SUI DUE GOLFI - MARINA DEL CANTONE - POSITANO
PRAIANO - VETTICA DI PRAIANO - VALLONE DI PRAIA
FIORDO DI FURORE - GROTTA DELLO SMERALDO
CONCA DEI MARINI - AMALFI - ATRANI - RAVELLO - SCALA
MAIORI AND MINORI - VIETRI SUL MARE

Project and editorial conception: Casa Editrice Bonechi
Publication Manager: Monica Bonechi
Cover, graphic design, lay-out: Sonia Gottardo
Maps: Belletti Editore, Misano Adriatico (Rimini)
Make-up: Fiorella Cipolletta
Editing: Anna Baldini

Text: Barbara Conti, Giovanna Magi, Giuliano Valdes, Casa Editrice Bonechi editorial staff.
Translation: Studio Comunicare, Firenze *and* Rhiannon Lewis.

CASA EDITRICE BONECHI, Via Cairoli 18/b
50131 Firenze
Tel +39 055576841 - Fax +39 0555000766

E-mail: bonechi@bonechi.it
Internet: www.bonechi.it

Printed in Italy by Centro Stampa Editoriale Bonechi.

Photographs from the archives of Casa Editrice Bonechi taken by A&5 Photo Studio, Giovanni Capodilupo, Paolo Giambone, MSA.

Other photographers:
A&5 Photo Studio: *pages 35 bottom, 61, 65 top;*
Atlantide/ Stefano Amantini: *pages 23 bottom, 31 bottom, 37 top;*
Atlantide/ Massimo Borchi: *pages 15 top, 46 bottom, 48, 49, 77 top, 78 centre, 79 bottom, 83 bottom;* Atlantide/ Guido Cozzi: *page 46 top;*
Gaetano Barone: *page 42 bottom;* Foto Amendola: *page 47 bottom;*
Foto Rainero/ Fadigati: *page 91 bottom;* Maurizio Fraschetti: *pages 11, 15 bottom, right, 30;* Francesco Giannoni: *pages 72, 73 a,b, 78 top;*
Ghigo Roli: *pages 26-27, 31 top, 83 top.*

ISBN 88-8029-936-0

* * *

Overlooking the Gulf of Sorrento.
Below, a fisherman from Sorrento repairs his nets, proof that an old seafaring tradition is very much alive.

INTRODUCTION

Of the countless jewels the region of Campania has to offer to the tourist, the Sorrentine peninsula is one of the finest. Geographically the peninsula is a branch of the Apennines, and juts out at right angles to the mountain chain, continuing under water all the way to the island of Capri, which it resembles geologically and structurally. Few other places in Italy can vaunt such variety in landscape, environment, history, culture, as does this portion of "Campania Felix", *set between the evocative gulfs of Naples and Salerno. The physical structure is determined first of all by the Lattari mountain chain, with a maximum height of 1,444 m. (Mt. Sant'Angelo), which joins the peninsula to the vast fertile plain of Nocera and the fruitful countryside of Sarno as far as the foothills of Vesuvius. Two roads, often narrow and winding but breathtakingly beautiful, permit us to explore the countryside and discover evocative towns, pleasant riparian resorts, idyllic lookout spots. This contact with a land and a people is a key to an understanding of this picturesque microcosmos of the Italian South. Two routes and two ambients – the coast of Sorrento and that of Amalfi – set face to face like jousting knights, but which are in the end united by the encompassing luminosity of the sun, the physical features of the landscape, harsh yet sweet, the infinite blue of the sky of Campania which seems to reflect the transparent shimmer of the sea.*

A panoramic shot of Amalfi.
Below, citrus fruits and hot red peppers, the colors and flavors of the Campania region.

The Tyrrhenian watershed, milder, gentler than the precipitous cliffs of Amalfi, is comprised of terraced slopes, suitable for agriculture and human settlements, which merge one into the other, both as well defined towns or scattered dwellings. Deep valleys furrowed by streams break the uniformity of the terraced Sorrentine watershed while the coastline is varied by the precipitous cliffs rising up over the bays and inlets. The city of Sorrento itself is situated upon the steep tufa cliffs which seem to form a natural bulwark.
At first sight the Amalfi watershed seems to be conditioned to a greater extent by the shape of the coastline, which is considerably steeper, and by the way in which the Lattari hills run right down to the coast, especially between Positano and Amalfi, leaving very little space for towns or crops. The only sites available for agriculture are at the points where the deep valleys that cut through the walls of rock that overlook the coast reach the ocean. The fascinating tortuous route that winds along the Amalfi coast on high presents us with idyllic seaside towns, charming panoramas and a landscape dominated by the flourishing Mediterranean bush and the traditional crops favored by a particularly mild and sunny microclimate. In the midst of this fablelike world is Amalfi, the ancient maritime republic, with its enviable patrimony of art, history and culture, a real "queen" of the various centers that are distinguished by their natural or urban setting.

SORRENTO

One of the finest of the many jewels which stud the peninsula of Sorrento is the city from which it took its name. Numbering somewhat under 18,000 inhabitants, the town is situated on a tufa terrace with sheer rocky cliffs which fall straight down to the sea. The amenities of the site and of the natural landscape, enhanced by the flourishing citrus groves, the immensity of the panorama over the gulf of Naples, Vesuvius and the Phlegraean Fields and the islands of the same name, the extraordinary transparency of the sea and an exceptionally clear blue sky, make this city one of the sanctuaries of international tourism. The well-equipped receptive structures, the high quality of the services offered, the range of opportunities for recreation, sport and culture have all contributed to its renown.

While the origins of its name merge with the myth of the sirens (Surrentum), no doubts exist as to the fact that man already lived here in Neolithic times. Probably founded as a Greek colony, it was successively under Etruscan, Syracusan and Samnite domination, until the arrival of the Romans which was greeted with little enthusiasm, and the inhabitants were always on the verge of rebellion. In Imperial times the city was one of the favorite vacation spots for Roman patricians. Subjected by the Goths and Byzantines, it succeeded in avoiding attempts at conquest by the Lombards but

A splendid view of the coast between Meta and Sorrento.

found itself forced to offer proud opposition to the Saracens and the citizens of Amalfi. Taken by the Normans in the first half of the 12th century, an uprising was attempted with the aid of the Republic of Pisa, until it was definitively subjugated by King Roger. It was hard tried by contrasts both within and without and had a tormented history of sieges and attempts at conquest, at least until the Parthenopaean Republic was constituted (late 18th cent.). The birthplace of Torquato Tasso, the famous 16thcentury poet, was already renowed as a residential center in the 18th century.

PIAZZA TASSO – The heart of the city is the central Piazza Tasso, one of the favorite sites for the evening promenade. Two statues stand in the tree-shaded square: the best-known is the one with a high base, the *Monument to Torquato Tasso*, the poet born in Sorrento on March 11, 1544, and who died in Rome on April 25, 1595, famous for his pastoral drama *Aminta* and the heroic poem *Jerusalem Delivered*. The sculpture was completed by G. Carli in 1870. The other statue, made by Tommaso Solari in 1879, depicts a blessing *St. Anthony Abbot*, the patron saint of Sorrento who found refuge here when the Lombards descended on the region.
Facing out on the square at the beginning of the *Corso Italia*, is the porticoed **Church of S. Maria del Carmine**. Inside are a fine tabernacle datable to the second half of the 18th century, and an allegorical painting on the ceiling, of Carmelite subject, painted in the first half of the 18th century by Onofrio Avellino.

PORT – The long shoreline of Sorrento is comprised of *Marina Grande*, where the infrastructures for seaside tourists, beaches and bathing establishments, are concentrated, and *Marina Piccola*. The latter is the largest maritime port of call of the city, used by motor-ships and hydrofoils of the navigation services of the gulf, in particular those headed for Naples and the neighboring picturesque island of

Sorrento, Piazza Tasso with the statue of the great writer is the heart of the city; the facade of the church of S. Maria del Carmine and the horse-drawn carriages that drive through city.

Capri. Dear to the great Roman Emperor Tiberius and a vast crowd of contemporary writers, the island is a must for the tourists who visit this fascinating stretch of the Campanian coast. The port of Sorrento is an ideal point of departure. The port structures, which are also equipped to receive the host of enthusiasts of the sea who drop anchor here during the summer, are protected by a long wharf.
For those who come via sea, Sorrento presents a particularly charming picture. The buildings, large and small, cling to the rocky tufa cliffs which drop sheer into a deep blue sea which shimmers and varies in color as the sun moves along its course. The whole coastline, with its steep cliffs, is dotted by numerous villas, dwellings and residences, in typically Mediterranean style, while the foliage of the maritime pines, the patches of Mediterranean bush, the lemon and citrus groves make the most of this rich luminous landscape setting.

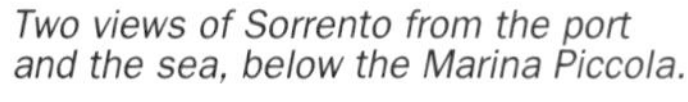

Two views of Sorrento from the port and the sea, below the Marina Piccola.

On the following pages: a view of the picturesque harbor of Marina Grande with the Marina Piccola in the background.

Sorrento, the fifteenth century loggia known as Sedile Dominova.

A detail of the richly decorated interior of the Sedile Dominova, with the coat of arms of Sorrento

SEDILE DOMINOVA – This curious name refers to one of the most characteristic buildings in the historical center of Sorrento. It is actually a 15th-century loggia, square in plan with large round Romanesque arches on its two open sides. They are supported on engaged columns with floral motives decorating the capitals.

Above and opposite page, bottom, two views of the unusual three story cathedral bell tower; the cell at the top once contained the bells.

The ensemble is dominated by an airy 17th-century The ensemble is dominated by an airy 17th-century dome, faced with twocolor tiles which confer an oriental air on the building. "Sedile" (or seat) is the name used to indicate a faction of the noble families of Sorrento who met here to deal with local problems. Inside, the 18th-century frescoes and the numerous coats of arms of the illustrious families of Sorrento who belonged to the "sedile" are of particular note and are set off by the fine decorative elements of the architecture.

Cathedral of Sorrento: the facade.

CATHEDRAL – The cathedral of Sorrento was first built around the 11th century but was completely rebuilt in the 15th century, on a scheme that was obviously of Renaissance inspiration. The building, with a modern facade in Gothic style, is accompanied by a curious bell tower in three stories, topped by a belfry originally meant to house the bells. The bell tower is decorated with a clock with a fine polychrome face, while the architectural elements of the base date to Roman times.

Cathedral of Sorrento: a detail of the majolica floor.

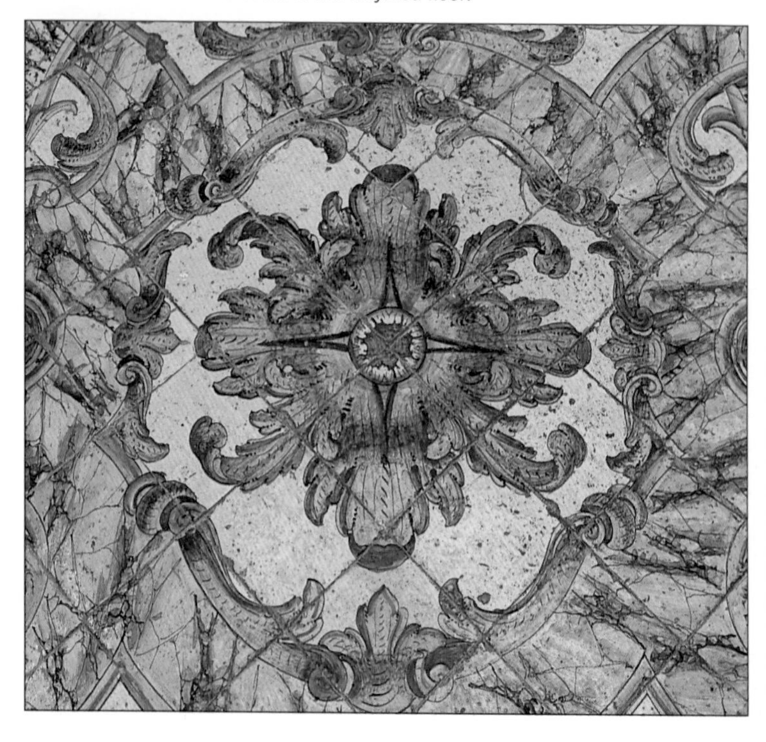

Cathedral of Sorrento: three views of the interior, with a detail of the ceiling, the wooden choir and a bas-relief.

The latin-cross **interior** is divided into a nave and two aisles by robust piers which support round arches. The interior abounds in marble decoration (some of Roman and medieval date) and is further enriched by the ceiling paintings in the nave by Malinconico (*Sorrentine Martyrs, Four Patron Bishop Saints*); those by Giacomo del Po, on the ceiling of the transept (*Assumption, St. Philip, St. James*); a fine 16th-century marble altar frontal, the marble pulpit and the bishop's throne, both of the 16th century.

CHURCH AND CLOISTER OF S FRANCESCO – This 18th-century church, dedicated to the saint from Assisi, stands near the *Villa Comunale*, a green and panoramic palm-shaded park. The verticality of the two-story facade is stressed by the number of pilaster strips. A large oculus is set into the upper tier while a statue is set above the center of the curvilinear tympanum on top. Artistically of greatest interest is a carved wooden door by a 16th-century artist.
The convent building annexed to the church is notable particularly for its small **Cloister**. Exceptionally fine stylistically, it frames a view of the bell tower with its characteristic spire, with masonry that in part dates to Roman times. Two sides of the cloister are articulated by octagonal columns with elegant capitals supporting round arches. The other two sides are striking in the interlacing of pointed arches, small columns and lunettes. This portion of the portico, 14th-century, reveals an obvious Arabic influence.

MUSEO CORREALE DI TERRANOVA – The collections of this interesting museum, installed in the *Palazzo Correale* (18th cent.), represent the fruits of the work of the count of Terranova, Alfredo Correale, and his brother Pompeo. They furnish an interesting cross-section of the minor artistic production of the late 17th – early 18th centuries, but also include paintings by Neapolitan artists, works from the classical and medieval periods.
On the *ground floor*: period furniture, ranging from the 16th to the 18th centuries; relics of Tasso; paintings of Neapolitan school (15th cent.); a collection of majolica from Italy and abroad; marble of Greek-Roman period; statues, sarcophagi, antique vases; inscriptions and architectural fragments. On the *first floor*: furniture and furnishings of various periods; paintings by local and foreign artists (of note Rubens, J. Jordaens, J. Brueghel); porcelain from Capodi-

Sorrento, the cloister of the eighteenth century church of S. Francesco, the monument to St. Anthony Abbot and the Museo Correale di Terranova.

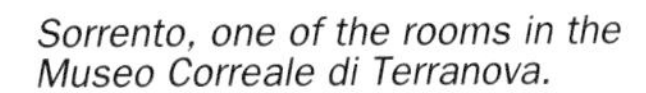

Sorrento, one of the rooms in the Museo Correale di Terranova.

monte and majolica. On the *second floor*, the series of period furnishings continues together with paintings by artists of the school of Posillipo. Lastly mention must be made of the collections of clocks and porcelain from Italy and Europe, together with old examples of local crafts.

ASPECTS OF THE HISTORICAL CENTER

When the tourist enters the labyrinth of alleys in the center of the city, he unexpectedly finds himself face to face with the real Sorrento. The narrow streets paved in stone are flanked by typical buildings with terraces and balconies. Sometimes signs of the medieval period are clearly evident in the slender brick and stone arches which join the old buildings.

Here is where one finds the typical shops with patient craftsmen who will show you the fruits of their labor and tempt you into making a "good buy". Elsewhere, with typically Mediterranean talent and fantasy, temporary stalls have sprung up which offer the most varied articles, from clothing to crafts, and the ever present "souvenir" to the bemused and curious tourist.

Sorrento, two typical craftsmen's shops specializing in sandals and cameos; fresh fish on sale in Via San Cesareo.

MARINA GRANDE – The picturesque *Via Marina Grande* which connects the historical center as such with the seashore known as Marina Grande below begins in the tree-shaded *Piazza della Vittoria*, near which a few Roman ruins seem to confirm the hypothesis that a temple consecrated to Venus once stood here. The narrow street winds along between arches and bypasses next to old buildings and gardens, ending in a stairway at the picturesque small port of Marina Grande.
The bathing establishments here still recall times past, with their brightly painted wooden cabins and the umbrellas all the colors of the rainbow set on piles and against the breakwater reefs.

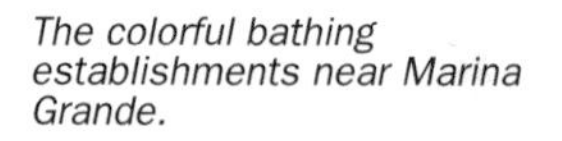

The colorful bathing establishments near Marina Grande.

Aerial view of the beach and harbor of Marina Grande.

In the midst of the many boats drawn up on the beach, the Sorrentine fishermen patiently repair their nets and hulls. At the center of the charming inlet, framed by the lovely landscape, the pleasure boats lie at anchor.

Marina Grande, two picturesque views of the port.

"Bagno della regina Giovanna", a deep, interesting fissure in the rock.

BAGNO DELLA REGINA GIOVANNA

After reaching the locality of Capo di Sorrento we recommend the pleasant outing to the fascinating *Punta del Capo*. The route leads through citrus groves and olive trees, and fine views are to be had. The sweeping panorama at the tip of the point embraces the peninsula, the city, the Plain of Sorrento, Punta Gradelle and Mount Faito whose sheer crags run down to the sea. The remains of a Roman building which strike the eye can be identified as foundation walls, with remains of other walls further inland, and ruins of masonry in *opus reticulatum* and of buildings for bathing purposes in the lower zone facing the sea.
A rather detailed description furnished by the Latin poet Publius Papinius Statius (45-96 A.D.) would seem to indicate that they were part of the **Villa of Pollio Felice**.
Nearby is the Bath of Queen Joan, or Bagno della Regina Giovanna, a picturesque cleft in the rock which permits sea water to pass through into a small pool, with clear shimmering water and ever-changing reflections.

Punta del Capo:
view of the ruins of the
ancient Villa of Pollio Felice.

Massa Lubrense, detail of a frieze on the facade of the church of S. Maria delle Grazie.

Massa Lubrense: a close-up of the Marina della Lobra dominated by the sanctuary below, right, the sanctuary's bell tower.

MASSA LUBRENSE

This charming holiday town and health resort takes the form of an amphitheatre on the hills above *Marina della Lobra*. The origins of the place name come from a combination of the early Middle Age word *massa* (which was used to indicate a group of rural dwellings and land) and the Latin expression *delubrum* (which referred to the presence of an ancient temple, probably dedicated to Minerva).
The **Church of S. Maria delle Grazie** (Our Lady of Grace) is situated in the higher zone of the built-up area. It was renovated in the second half of the 18th century and has a valuable majolica pavement and a painting of *Our Lady of Grace* by Andrea da Salerno. Marina della Lobra is a picturesque fishing village with well-organized moorings for tourist boats and is the location of the 16th-century **Sanctuary of Santa Maria "della Lobra"** which stands on the site occupied by previous places of worship dating back to pagan time. It has a majolica floor, a coffered ceiling and a wooden 18th century *Crucifix*.

Preceding pages: aerial view of Punta Campanella, the farthest cape on the Sorrento Peninsula, facing Capri; from here the eye can wander along the entire Amalfi Coast.

Sant'Agata sui due Golfi: above a panoramic view of the Salerno side; below, looking towards the Piano di Sorrento, Punta Gradelle and the Vesuvius.

SANT'AGATA SUI DUE GOLFI

This pleasant panoramic locality is situated on a high ridge in the lower portion of the peninsula of Sorrento. It is a holiday resort, is well-frequented by tourists, and from here there is an extensive view towards the gulfs of Naples and Sorrento which gives it its name.
The **Church of S. Maria delle Grazie** is the 17th-century Parish Church and contains 16th- and 17th-century paintings, and a notable main altar which was brought here from a Neapolitan church at the beginning of the 19th century. This is made out of multicolored marble interspersed with semi-precious stones and mother-of-pearl and is the work of 16th-century Florentine artists. The place of major interest to tourists, however, is the **Desert**; originally a Carmelite hermitage which was later used as an orphanage, it is famous for the beautiful sweeping panorama which can be admired from the terrace and which overlooks the two bays, Vesuvius, the Sorrento peninsula and the lovely island of Capri.

MARINA DEL CANTONE

Marina del Cantone is about five kilometers from S. Agata sui due Golfi, the marvelous terminus of a road that winds down to the sea through vineyards and citrus groves. A farflung panorama of the spacious gulf of Positano is available from the beach, the largest in the Sorrentine peninsula.
The characteristic crags of *Li Galli* stand opposite Marina del Cantone.

They are also known as Isole Sirenuse, for according to legend this is where the mythical sirens who enchanted Ulysses lived. However, with typically Neapolitan fantasy, local folklore has invented an addition to the tale, in which the sirens were beautiful women who loved to dance, in particular the tarantella, and whose legs were transformed into flippers by the envious Graces.
Legend aside, the crags nowadays are the goal of outings by boat: the largest is known as Gallo Lungo and the others, for their forms, are called the Castelluccia and the Rotonda; somewhat apart, the rock of Vetara rises from the water. But even for those who prefer to stay on the beach, the beauties of a clean sea and the sheer drop of the coast amply compensate. To the right of the town lies the *Tower of Montalto*, an old lookout over the open sea.

Two lovely views of Marina del Cantone and its popular beaches; below, an aerial view of the Li Galli rocks from where the Sirens supposedly sang to Ulysses and his men.

TOWARDS POSITANO

The road that leads from Marina del Cantone to Positano passes by S. Agata sui due Golfi, a popular vacation resort, in a magnificent panoramic site between the Gulf of Naples and that of Salerno, the Sorrentine peninsula and Capri. Here one enters state highway 163, known as ***"Nastro Azzurro"*** *(Blue Ribbon) because of the color of the sea which is always in sight; the road joins Salerno and S. Agata before moving down towards the Amalfi coast.*
From the point of view of scenery the itinerary is outstanding: each of the many curves holds a surprise. Views of the coastline of Sorrento alternate with that of Amalfi; in the distance the ridge of Mount Faito is marked by rows of firs; up closer, Monte S. Angelo di Meta comes into sight and on clear days the cone of Vesuvius is visible above a col. The vast plain of Sorrento stretches out as far as the eye can see, with peaceful towns in the midst of green olive and citrus groves.
At Colli di S. Pietro the road runs down to the sea and the marvelous panorama of the gulf of Salerno, from its furthest point up to Capo Sottile, spreads out before our eyes.
The coast is characterized by broad fissures such as at Grotta Matera, where the seaslips in past the rocks, or the Vallone dello Scaricatore. The Amalfi Coast, a high rocky rampart overhanging the sea, begins here, one

State road n.163 that links Salerno and Sant'Agata, and then goes down to the Amalfi Coast, is known as the "Blue Ribbon" and follows the most breathtaking landscapes.

of the most popular tourist attractions of the Italian peninsula. In the last stretch before Positano the road passes through a broad deep valley with limestone spires and towers on high, then under the "Ponte dei Libri", in a deep cleft in the rock, with a tall spire on either side. The road twists along, high above the sea, and, after a short descent, arrives at the Belvedere of Positano, from which a glimpse of the picturesque city is to be had.

Following pages: a panorama of Positano, with the tiled dome of the church of S.Maria Assunta in the center.

POSITANO

One of the most famous vacation spots on the coast, Positano is situated in a splendid gorge which gradually widens out as it moves towards the sea.
From stepped terraces, set against Mount Comune on the west and Mount S. Angelo ai Tre Pizzi on the east, the built-up area overlooks a small beach.
One of the characteristic features of Positano is the architecture of the houses: cubes, painted white, pink, red, orange, almost all with a small porch in front, some with a spherical dome.
The entire built-up area is surrounded by green palm and citrus groves, which makes it particularly delightful.

Aerial view of the beach at Positano, the splendid sea and countless houses perched on the cliffs that slope down to the shore.

Steep stairways, squeezed in between the houses, serve as roads; those who live in Positano are used to climbing up and down all day long and it is said that when the time comes for them to climb the stairs to Paradise it will be child's play. It was this feature which led the famous painter Paul Klee to define Positano as "the only place in the world conceived of on a vertical rather than a horizontal axis". The singer Roberto Murolo also owes his fame to the stairs of Positano, stairs which inspired his "Scalinatella".

But while the tourist may feel his legs during his visit to the city, these alleys provide unbelievably beautiful views that slope down to an intensely blue sea, of striking beauty.

A GLANCE AT THE PAST – According to tradition, Positano was founded by inhabitants of Paestum, from whom they may have inherited the name of *Pestano* or *Pesitano*, who were seeking refuge in the area after their city had been destroyed by the Saracens. But it is more likely that the name derives from the *Posidii* family, who possessed lands in the area.
The development of Positano began in the period of the Maritime Republics. Until then the city had been simply a possession of the abbey of S. Vito, and in this feudal bond commercial development was not contemplated.
Eventually Positano rebelled and even though it rivalled with Amalfi made great headway when it succeeded in organizing a fleet which plied the entire Mediterranean and established trading centers everywhere.
Like all centers on the Amalfi coast, Positano was frequently attacked from the sea. The three lookout towers in strategic positions around the town still today testify to the many Saracen incursions.
The decline of Positano was gradual and was bound to the vicissitudes of the coastal centers which originally profitted from their proximity to Amalfi but which followed in its fate. In the 18th century Positano was abandoned by most of its inhabitants and in effect was not reborn until the 20th century. Today it owes its fortune above all to tourism, for which numerous activities and comfortable infrastructures have been developed.
There are few real roads in Positano, as previously stated: *Via Pasitea*, which leaves the state highway and winds along into the village, and *Via Mulini*, which leads to the Piazza Flavio Gioia. Otherwise it is an intricate network of small stairways which connect houses and gardens.

The coast near Positano: above, the Li Galli rocks in the background and the Clavel tower in the foreground at the end of the Fornillo beach; below: another watchtower near Positano.

Two picturesque shots of the center of Positano.

On these pages, different views of the church of S. Maria Assunta that dominates the village of Positano.

THE CHURCH OF S. MARIA ASSUNTA – The landscape of Pos tano is dominated by the parish church of S. Maria Assunta, wit its great tiled **dome**: inside, pilasters divide the nave from th two side aisles. It contains a *Circumcision* of the late 16th centu ry by Fabrizio Santafede, and a 13th-century panel in Byzar tine style, depicting the *Madonna and Child*. To be noted, i the bell tower, a medieval bas-relief of a sea monster, fish es and a fox.

In practically no time one goes down from the piazza t the *Marina Grande* with a strand bordered by cliffs There are three beaches west of Marina: *La Porta*, *Ci micello* and *Arienzo*.

Colorful Mediterranean houses dot the Positano panorama; an unusual view of the small beach.

The village, beaches and the sea seen from the terrace of a restaurant.

LA PORTA – The cave of La Porta (Grotta La Porta) near the inhabited center, 200 meters below the state highway for Amalfi, merits particular attention. Prehistoric man lived in this ancient cavern, originally much larger than it is now, in the Upper Palaeolithic period (circa 15,000 years ago) and in the Mesolithic period (10,000 years ago). Implements for hunting and for daily use, as well as the remains of land and sea molluscs which were used as food, have been found here. Why these cave-dwellers left is a mystery. It is likely that they had to move elsewhere when part of the grotto caved in.

TOURIST CITY – In the early 1920s and 1930s Positano was an oasis for intellectuals and artists, who favored it for vacations and as the setting for their encounters. When these periods were protracted in time, as was often the case, Positano was completely transformed and soon acquired renown as one of the most elegant of Italian intellectual salons.
The first to "colonize" it in this sense were the Russians, including the great choreographer and ballet dancer Massine, and then Gorki and Lenin.
Other famous personalities, such as Picasso and Cocteau, soon followed suit. The atmosphere of the city is still intact, even today. It is known that Eduardo de Filippo, famous Italian playwright, invented some of his best lines here. The hotel whose clientele includes the more notable guests of the coast, nobility, artists, actors or directors, is the "San Pietro".
Culturally something is always going on in Positano, and the tourist has but to choose. During the summer there is the *Premio Positano for dance*; in September the *Music Festival*, and in other periods painting exhibitions are frequently organized, often centered on the theme of the local landscape, natural marvels as well as architectural aspects.
The omnipresent typical locales and shops sell local craft products such as decorated tiles and pottery, objects in wood, lace, wine. It must not be forgotten that Positano owes some of its success and fame to the brightly-colored gypsy-style summer clothes which are to be found just about everywhere in the shops of the city. Made of large kerchiefs, they can be worn either by adults or children, and correspond as much to elite as to popular taste. Currently tourism is undoubtedly the most important source of income for the inhabitants of Positano: thanks to its picturesque position, its climate and the comfortable hotels the city is one of the most popular on the coast. There is also a good choice of restaurants which offer local specialities: for a moderate price one can have fresh fish (fishing is another important item in the economy of the area) as well as excellent agricultural products from the interior: plump olives, citrus fruits to be eaten sliced with nothing but a sprinkling of sugar, sweet figs.

Positano, Hotel San Pietro seen from above and a panoramic view of Positano from a bench with a maiolica back at the famous hotel.

A picturesque area of Positano, with the lavish villas members of the international jet-set have built in this little corner of paradise.

On these pages, the breathtaking, untamed landscapes near Positano.

SURROUNDINGS OF POSITANO – Outings on foot can be made from Positano: two kilometers away, along the road to Sorrento, of particular interest is the previously mentioned "*Ponte dei Libri*" which arches over a deep valley in a striking location, with a high spire at either side.
At a distance of about two and a half kilometers is the village of *Montepertuso*, and not far from this, *Nocelle*: both quite charming.
Breathtaking panoramas, with the sea in the background, framed by sheer cliffs and cut by deep bays, can be had along small roads in the mountains of S. Angelo ai Tre Pizzi and Comune, which rise to a height of respectively 1400 m. and 900 m.

THE AMALFI COAST

The Amalfi coast is characterized by its location high over the sea, split and eroded in various points, with ravines and grottoes. Rocky and wild, it is an endless sequence of sharp rocks, spires, towers that move down towards the sea and on which the hand of man has laid out a series of terraces planted with olives, citrus trees, vineyards.
*Towards the interior the ridge of the Lattari hills acts as backdrop. The name goes back to Roman times, perhaps because of the great quantity of milk (*latte *in Italian) which was produced here.*
Travelling from Positano towards Amalfi, the road moves inland in order to go round the Vallone of Positano. On high is the Natural Arch, a large opening in the rock below Monte S. Angelo, particularly evocative in the morning when the rays of the sun shine through. After crossing a small river, the road turns back to the sea. From here on it is one ravine after another, one cliff after the other, while Positano appears and disappears from sight as one curve after the other is rounded.
The clearing behind the small church of S. Pietro which stands on the point of the same name offers a splendid view of the gulf, from Punta Campanella to Capo Sottile. Further on, the road reveals even more sweeping panoramas, which embrace the island of Capri, the crags of the Faraglioni and the small Li Galli islands. The coast here has, not without reason, often been called "divine" to stress its unusual qualities. The landscape on the other side of the road, inland, should also be noted, with green hills which often provide the traveler with a reason for stopping. The plateau of Agérola is full of chestnut woods and large open meadows. The itinerary along the coast is, in a sense, a rediscovery of the original dominion of the Maritime Republic of Amalfi, which went from Positano to Cetera and the ridge of the Lattari hills.
As we have said, the hand of man has created a series of terraces on this steep land, on which the houses have been placed, overlooking one of the cleanest seas in Italy, apparently clinging to inaccessible rocks. As a result the towns consist of houses set one above the other, with serpentine alleys, and crops grown on hard-won artificial fields. Fishing was originally the only activity, but now agriculture has also been developed and the local population has been described as having "one foot in the boat, the other in the vineyard".

Two typical views of the Amalfi Coast with the old watchtowers projecting over the water, and the coast seen from the cliffs.

The Vallone di Praia seen from above.

VETTICA DI PRAIANO

The inhabited center of Vettica Maggiore or Vettica di Praiano is situated about 23 kilometers from Positano. A small narrow road leads from this picturesque bathing village to the beach with cliffs on either side.
Like the other towns in the area, Vettica was included in the territory of the ancient Maritime Republic of Amalfi, and its fate was that of Amalfi as it flourished and then went into an inevitable decline. Now, in addition to tourism, Vettica depends on fishing, which has always been a profitable activity, and agricultural products of which it can be justly proud: figs, carobs, citrus fruits, grapes.
The climate, as in the rest of the Sorrentine peninsula, is one of the mildest in Italy. In winter the average temperature is above 10° centigrade while in July-August the thermometer rarely goes higher than 25° centigrade, still another reason for staying in this charming town.
Of particular interest from the point of view of architecture is the **parish church of S. Gennaro**, rebuilt at the end of the 16th century on an older construction, with a dome that is tiled like all the others in the area. The bell tower, built in the 18th century, is octagonal at the top with a small tiled dome.
The interior has a nave and two aisles, divided by pilasters, and with interesting paintings of religious subjects, dating to the 16th and 17th centuries. They include a *Martyrdom of S. Bartholomew* by Giovanni Bernardo Lama, and a *Holy Family* which, together with others, decorates the altars in the side chapels.
The small square in front of the church offers the spectacle of Positano and the Faraglioni. Like many other localities of the Sorrentine peninsula, Vettica is to be appreciated in particular for the peace and quiet it offers: the clean sea which is still full of fish and suitable for scuba diving; the simplicity of life and the candor of the inhabitants; a place such as is rarely found today, where certain aspects of life such as good food and healthy air still matter.

The parish church of S. Gennaro at Vettica di Praiano.

VALLONE DI PRAIA

One of the most characteristic of the many fiords which cut the Amalfi Coast is the Vallone di Praia, a broad fissure surrounded by tall cliffs, on the skirts of which small houses have been built for the local fishermen.
A lane cut into the rock leads from the state highway down into the deep valley and terminates at the charming small beach with its crystal-clear sea, well worth a halt. As is often the case along this stretch of coast, nature looks wild and still uncontaminated by man. The deep valleys like Praia are the result of the geological nature of the terrain which in this particular part of the peninsula is always in movement, continuously rising or sinking as much as a meter per year.
The rather crumbly rock is constantly subject to erosion by the waves of the sea and bizzarre forms remain when sections collapse, furnishing a unique spectacle.
The rock which splits off the mountain is finely crushed and is deposited on the bottom of the sea, eventually forming the many beaches, both small and large, to be found in the area.
Often the torrents that flow down from the mountain cut through the rock on their way to the sea, an obvious explanation for the many ravines and fiords along the coast.

Two shots of the Vallone di Praia, one of the most characteristic little spots along the Amalfi Coast.

PRAIANO

This vacation spot on the Sorrentine peninsula is situated at the base of the Lattari hills, on a rampart of Monte S. Angelo ai Tre Pizzi, which juts out into the sea with Capo Sottile.
It is said the name derives from *Plagianum* or *Pelagianum*, the peoples who according to legend first inhabited the site.
At the time of the Maritime Republic, Praiano was world famous for its silk industry, which provided the people with comfort and prosperity. Its climate led the Doges of the Republic to choose the town as their holiday resort, which naturally augmented its prestige in the course of the centuries. Charles I of Anjou had the University built, a confirmation of the culture achieved at the time by the town.
Praiano shared the fate of the Maritime Republic with Amalfi. After its fall, the small town continued its activities, in particular fishing which supplied the surrounding area.

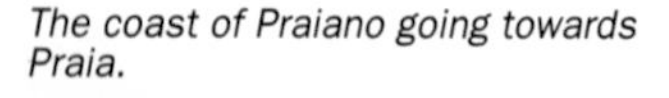

The coast of Praiano going towards Praia.

Even now around fifty small concerns make their living from this activity and the transformation of the catch. The citrus fruits of the area, most of which are exported, are also famous throughout the world.
Tourism is however the most dynamic factor in the local economy and in recent years comfortable family-style hotels and restaurants have gone up in Praiano and the surrounding towns.
The houses are scattered here and there on the slope which drops steeply down to the sea, with the ribbon of the state highway which runs along the Amalfi Coast above.

A bird's eye view of the village of Praia perched on steep slopes.

The **parish church of S. Luca**, at the top of the town, is rather interesting even though the exterior is the result of various remodelings. The interior, with a nave and two aisles, has various canvases that have been attributed to Giovanni Bernardo Lama, a 16th-century painter: a *Madonna and Child between St. Luke and St. Francis of Paola*, a *Madonna del Carmine*, a *Madonna del Buon Consiglio* and a *Circumcision*. Not to be overlooked in the sacristy is the *silver bust of St. Luke*, containing relics of the patron saint of Praiano. Celebrations in his honor take place in the first two weeks of July.
The old lookout tower is still visible near the town, built directly on the rock.

Two views of the impressive Fiordo di Furore near Marina di Praia.

FIORDO DI FURORE

The mention of fiords always brings to mind Scandinavia and the awe-inspiring bays along the coast. But similar examples of erosion, where the earth in the course of centuries has been scooped out by the never-ceasing action of the water, can be found in Italy as well. One of these is on the Amalfi Coast, where, as elsewhere on this delightful peninsula, nature appears at her wildest, contrasting with the charming villages, the beautifully kept terraces with their crops, the balmy inviting sea. The fiord of Furore is about 14 kilometers from Positano, near Marina di Praia, and the road crosses it on a high viaduct. The ravine was formed by a torrent which no longer has much water and which ran down from the uplands of Agérola.
A small path, a bit upstream from the viaduct, makes it possible to enter this fascinating gorge on foot. Interesting outings can be undertaken from

Looking down from the top of the Fiordo di Furore; below, the Emerald Grotto that can be toured in small boats.

the fiord: a path which begins at the viaduct and is in large part cut out of the rock in steps, leads in two hours on foot first to the picturesque group of houses known as S. Elia, and then to the village of Furore, both of which are in the direction of the upland of Agérola.
The view from these villages in the interior is endless, and looks out over an intensely blue ocean.
The surrounding countryside is characterized by the vineyards which produce the typical local wine, known as "Gran Furore Divina Costiera".
Once upon a time this hinterland was also part of the Maritime Republic, and furnished agricultural products to the cities on the coast, receiving in return fish and goods from the East and other ports on the Mediterranean.
In the first half of this century, the commune was aggregated to Conca dei Marini, but it then once more became autonomous permitting the inhabitants a greater autonomy and a shrewder management of the resources.

GROTTA DELLO SMERALDO

It should come as no surprise that the Emerald Grotto, as the cave at *Capo Conca dei Marini* is known, takes its name from the brilliant green reflections in the water when the sun filters through inside. The light is also reflected on the walls, unreal and magical. This sensation is enhanced by the irregular form of the walls and the numerous stalagmites and stalagtites.
A stairway cut into the rock leads directly from the highway to the cave, but to make it even easier an elevator has been installed. This unbelievable grotto can thus be seen by all: an entrance fee is paid and boats take the visitor inside.
Emerald Grotto was discovered in 1932: it measures 60 by 30 meters, with a maximum height above water of 24 meters. Originally the cave was dry and was flooded when the coast of the entire Sorrentine peninsula subsided.
Some of the stalagmites have fused during the centuries and form columns about 10 meters high: a natural temple of gigantic size. Since the opening to the outside is below sea level, the light is refracted and assumes this unique color.
Recently a ceramic crêche has been set at the bottom of the cave, about 4 meters under water, testifying to the genuine faith of the local inhabitants.

CONCA DEI MARINI

Conca dei Marini is one of the many tranquil vacation spots scattered along the Amalfi Coast. It is reached by following the state highway along the coast, and turning off at the cape of the same name.
Once the town was much more important than might be supposed from its present peaceful aspect. Its merchant ships, in fact, were active throughout the Mediterranean, and brought wealth and prestige to the inhabitants. During the Maritime Republic, it became Amalfi's most important naval base.
Nowadays the major resource is tourism and Conca dei Marini is well equipped with good hotels and typical restaurants. The position of the town is quite pleasing thanks to the panorama which spreads out before the tourist's eyes.
Torre di Conca, erected in the 16th century as a watchtower between the two bays of Praiano and Amalfi, rises up on Capo Conca. Until relatively recently this patch of land was used by the inhabitants of Conca as a cemetery.
The numerous interesting rustic houses in the town are covered by barrel vaults, cross or pavillion vaulting, of Eastern inspiration.
The former convent of S. Rosa, now a hotel, is another example of this architectural style. It is covered by several barrel vaults set above still another barrel vault creating an air chamber in between which serves as insulation for the rooms inside.
A vast panorama is to be had from the square in front of S. Rosa, overlooking the town.
The houses clinging to the steep slope of the rocky ramparts which drop straight down to the sea from the uplands of Agérola also play a part in making the whole city picturesque.
The local inhabitants say that one of the rocky spurs which embrace the town looks like a Madonna and Child. This is another example of how nature in these places has stimulated the imagination.
The famous American novelist John Steinbeck lived here at length, fascinated by the natural surroundings. His writings show that he was particularly struck by the boats that went out to sea at night with large lights on their prows, to fish sardines and squid all night long with their lights dotting the sea to the edge of the horizon.

A beautiful view looking towards Capo di Conca.

The Amalfi Coast seem from Conca dei Marini, one of the most tranquil spots on the coast.

AMALFI

The coat of arms of Amalfi, together with those of Venice, Genoa and Pisa, is depicted at the center of the flag of the Italian navy. Amalfi is one of the oldest centers in the area and documents testify to its existence as early as the 8th century A.D. But its fortunes came with the dominion of Constantinople: the Byzantine troops first helped Amalfi to defeat the Lombards, and then the remoteness of the government made autonomy possible. Economically this was a period of great development. Amalfi soon had a flourishing fleet which defeated the Saracens and established its position as queen of the Mediterranean. Even though, thanks to a conspiracy, the Lombards succeeded in conquering the city at the end of the ninth century, the inhabitants of Amalfi soon rebelled, and once they had regained possession of the inhabited center, elected one of their members as head with the title of "comes"*: independence had truly been achieved, and the city became a free republic, until 1137.*

The duchy of Amalfi embraced the entire zone between Sorrento, Salerno and the Lattari hills: for a long time it played a leading role both in commerce and in the wars which raged along the southern coasts. In 849 the Saracens were defeated as they were preparing to attack Rome; in 920 with its aid Reggio Calabria was freed from this oppressing presence. In exchange for favors to Louis II, Amalfi received dominion over the island of Capri.

Trade and commerce brought in great wealth throughout the 11th century: spices, perfumes, precious textiles, carpets arrived from the Orient.

Trade regulations throughout the Mediterranean were based on the maritime laws of Amalfi, the so-called Tavole Amalfitane (Amalfi Tables), of which a copy is in the Town Hall. The downfall of the city after the 11th century was due to internecine struggles: the Prince of Salerno, with the aid of the Normans, took over the Republic and Sorrento. Later, having passed to the Norman dynasty, Amalfi enjoyed a certain amount of liberty, at least administrative, until 1131. Exhausted by struggles and disagreements among the citizens themselves, it was attacked by its ancient marine rival Pisa, in 1135 and in 1137, and conquered. Its commercial wealth continued for some time, but liberty had definitely been shelved. Amalfi became the feud, with part of its original territory, of the Colonna, later of the Orsini, and finally of the Piccolomini: nothing else of note took place and it remained in their possession until 1582.

Masaniello, the fisherman who led a popular uprising against the Spanish government, was born in Amalfi in 1623. He succeeded in negotiating with the viceroy of Naples, imposing conditions and getting a tax on fruit and vegetables, which weighed heavily on the poorer people, abolished. As a result he was nominated captain by the people but, perhaps because his rise

One of the three symbols in the Amalfi coat of arms, and the lively ceramic panels decorating the City Hall.

had been so sudden, he began to give signs of instability and to appear in public with the powerful of the viceroyalty. Exasperated by his behaviour, those who had elected him, killed him.
A late 18th-century scholar noted: "Amalfi at present is a tiny city in a tiny corner among the rocks of the coast". Evidently at the time nothing was left of its antique greatness nor of the great fleet which had written its name in the history of the Mediterranean and of Europe.

THE CITY – The port gradually shrank in size and in the end completely disappeared, swallowed up by the erosion along the coast.
Today its splendid position between the mountains and the sea make the city one of the most characteristic panoramas on the Amalfi coast: its steep covered lanes, almost like corridors rather than real streets, are famous throughout the world, and often appear in box-office films.
Unfortunately little remains of the original town, for it was almost razed to the ground by tidal waves that struck in 1013 and in 1343. All that is left of its antique magnificence, in addition to its almost tangible aura, is the **Duomo** or **Cathedral**, with its spectacular staircase and the splendid adjoining **cloister**, the **Arsenals of the Republic**, and the **convent of the Cappuccini**.

A broad view of the city of Amalfi.

The city's architecture and beaches. Amalfi is not merely an art city: it is renowned for its well-equipped bathing establishments, beautiful beaches and many restaurants.

The first thing that strikes the visitor to Amalfi is the color: The first thing that strikes the visitor to Amalfi is the color: boats in red and green, striped blue and white, with the blue-green note of the sea, the backdrop of the houses with the orange and pink splashes of the flowers climbing up their walls, and the green of the gardens.
Any number of outstanding figures in the fields of art, theater, music, have come to Amalfi for a visit, which may even have stretched out to several months. Boccaccio, Longfellow, Victor Hugo, Ibsen, Wagner, D'Annunzio, Quasimodo are only a few of the most famous names.
While nowadays tourists arrive in droves, for centuries the Amalfi Coast and Amalfi were for the privileged few, for getting there was anything but easy, and the safest way was a tiring trip by sea.

In the 19th century Ferdinand of Bourbon, king of Naples, had the road that joins Vietri to Positano built. This is still the road that the present-day tourist uses to reach Amalfi, following the lay of the mountains on one side, while the other side falls straight down to the sea. In 1935 the American novelist John Steinbeck could not get over the reckless drivers who sped along the road.

The poetical nostalgia felt by many of those who have lived in Amalfi may in part derive from the fact that some of the hotels they stayed in, such as the Luna and the Cappuccini, were convents in the 13th century. For Ibsen and Wagner the atmosphere provided just the right note and allowed them to finish their most famous works, as noted in the two plaques in the Hotel Luna. Permission to visit these places is kindly given. In the 13th century when the Hotel Luna was a convent it belonged to the Franciscans, and the cloister of that time still stands complete with its characteristic pointed arches and its wellhead, set, like a small gem, at the center. The annex of the hotel also has an unusual history, for it was once an old watchtower, used to give the alarm when enemy ships, above all Saracen, were sighted still far out to sea so that the citizens could prepare for the attack.

At the end of the Via Camera, which begins at Piazza Flavio Gioia, is the Albergo Cappuccini, erected in 1212 on the site of a small church which dated back to before the 10th century.

Initially the convent was entrusted to the Cistercians. When they abandoned it, it passed to the Capuchins, from whence its name. The lovely cloister with a magnificent view of all Amalfi and the charm of its architecture is also open to the public.

The typical seafaring village of the oldest Italian Maritime Republic.

PIAZZA DEL DUOMO – The Piazza Duomo is at the center of the city and contains a Baroque **fountain** known as of the People or of St. Andrew (del Popolo or S. Andrea), erected in 1760. The large cartouches on the base are always covered with fresh flowers, placed there by the townsfolk as a sign of their devotion to the saint. Legend says that he saved Amalfi from the Saracens in 1544 in answer to the fervent prayers of the entire population, terrorized at the sight of ships arriving from afar.

St. Andrew raised a tempest at sea which forced the invaders to turn back after having lost ships and men. The feat is solemnly remembered on June 27th with devout processions and celebrations, during which the statue of the saint is carried up to the sea on the shoulders of the members of the Confraternity entrusted with the celebrations, dressed in white.

The silver statue, two and a half meters high and extremely heavy, is then handed over to the local fishermen who take it back to the Cathedral, with great fatigue, and carry it up the entrance staircase. The residents of Amalfi have transformed the religious celebration into a moment of joy and collective gaiety in which the entire population takes part, with choirs and music, and candlelight processions on the neighboring mountains and the beach.

Amalfi, Piazza del Duomo: the impressive fountain of St. Andrew.

A detail of the fountain of St. Andrew and a view of Piazza del Duomo.

THE CATHEDRAL – The cathedral is dedicated to St. Andrew. Originally constructed in the 9th century, it was repeatedly remodelled. Enlarged in the 10th century, rebuilt in Arabic-Norman forms in the 13th, remodelled in the 16th and 17th centuries, it was once more renovated, between 1701 and 1731. The **facade** was damaged in 1861, and was rebuilt from the few fragments which might give an idea of the original 13th-century forms.
The **bell tower** is oddly separated from the facade of the Cathedral and not in line with the main facade. Artistically outstanding, it is a survivor of the original cathedral, and was begun in 1180 and finished about a century later. The two- and three-light openings which lighten the structure are surmounted by a crowning of interlacing arches, which recall the Arabic style. The majolica covering in yellow and green is unusual.
The story of the bell tower is also part of the story of the people of Amalfi for they barricaded themselves here in 1389 when they were resisting the troops of Louis of Anjou, whom they managed to repulse after repeated attempts.
A long **flight** of 62 steps must be climbed to get to the cathedral but the evocative Gothic atrium, the reflection of light on the lively facade with its ornamental motives of Byzantine, Arab, Norman derivation make it well worth the effort.
Of particular note are the *bronze doors* which lead to the interior. They were cast in Constantinople in the 11th century and donated to the Cathedral of Amalfi by Pantaleone di Mauro Comite (as mentioned in an inscription), a citizen of Amalfi whose name is bound to the foundation of the order of the Knights of St. John, in Jerusalem, where he had founded a hospital.
The bas-relief on the doors depicts *Christ*, the *Madonna, Saint Andrew and St. Peter*. Traces, even though slight, of the original silvering with which it was once entirely covered are still visible.
On either side of the portal are frescoes with *scenes from the life of Christ and of St. Andrew*, which were painted by Paolo Vetri in 1929, on designs by Domenico Morelli.

The magnificent cathedral of Amalfi dedicated to St. Andrew, patron saint of the city. The cathedral is famous for its facade that has obvious references to the Byzantine, Moorish and Norman styles

The majestic **interior**, also renovated, is Baroque in form: some of the columns which separate the nave from the side aisles are original. Moreover the rich carved and painted *coffered ceiling* makes the Cathedral a strong calling card. The *high altar* is particularly beautiful. The ambos on either side, decorated with mosaic fragments, belonged to the old church and date to the 13th century.
Steps in the right aisle lead down into the *crypt* which is also quite haunting. It dates to 1253 and in the 18th century was divided into the two aisles it has today. It is here that the sculpture of greatest importance from the historical-artistic point of view is to be found: in fact, the *altar* is by Domenico Fontana, while the *marble statues of St. Stephen and St. Laurence* are by Pietro Bernini. The body of St. Andrew, venerated as a relic, is preserved under the altar. It was brought here from Constantinople in 1208 in answer to popular devotion, thanks to the cardinal of Amalfi, Pietro Capuano.
The bones of the Saint continually exude a liquid substance, here called "the manna of St. Andrew", which is said to have miraculous virtues.
From the right aisle there is also access to the *Chapel of the Crucifix*, the best preserved part of the entire building. The historiated capitals and the airy pointed arches give us an idea of what the church must have been like when it was first built, when nothing else troubled the perfection of the forms.

Amalfi, the cathedral: the beautiful bronze door, and the Gothic style atrium.

The lavish Baroque interior of the Amalfi cathedral, and the sixteenth century of the crypt with statues by Bernini

Amalfi, the marvelous Chiostro del Paradiso adjacent to the cathedral reveals distinct Moorish influence.

Fragments of Romanesque and Medieval frescoes and mosaics are conserved in the Chiostro del Paradiso.

CLOISTER OF PARADISE – Returning to the atrium of the Cathedral, on the left, is the entrance to the marvelous cloister, so peerlessly harmonious that it is called the "Chiostro del Paradiso" (Cloister of Paradise). The influence of the Arab world on Amalfi, and on the tastes of its people, is quite evident here. One cannot but be aware on entering this airy cloister of the purely eastern elegance of the slender white columns, with arches that are so pointed that they do not resemble the Gothic arch of the European church, but the one to be found in the atrium of a Near Eastern palace. The plants at the center of the cloister also enhance this effect: palms are more at home in oriental gardens than in Italian ones. The cloister was built in 1266 by the bishop of Amalfi, Filippo Augustoriccio, and initially served as cemetery for the most illustrious citizens of Amalfi. At present it contains material from the Roman and medieval periods: Roman sarcophagi decorated with bas-reliefs of different subjects; arches and other fragments of the original facade of the Duomo, decorated in mosaic. Arabic influence is evident in the stylized geometric designs.

Of particular note artistically is a large fresco with the *Crucifixion*, painted around 1330 by Roberto d'Oderi-

sio, a Neapolitan painter who was active throughout the Sorrentine peninsula. The cathedrals of Ravello, Salerno, and Scala, all contain frescoes or panels of religious subjects commissioned to this painter by the wealthy and devout families of the zone.
Documentary evidence exists testifying to how much the king of Naples Carlo Durazzo appreciated Roberto. In fact he was named court painter in 1302 and given the right to live there, a privilege in precedence conceded only to Giotto. And it was by none other than Giotto, who sojourned in Naples from 1329 to 1333, that Roberto was influenced, as is evident in the Amalfi fresco of the Crucifixion: the figures are massive and filled with pathos, the soldiers under the Cross with their horses construct the space they stand in.
If one desires to continue the visit of this splendid city after having seen the Cathedral, one can follow Corso Roma, one of the principal streets of Amalfi, particularly charming because it opens seawards.

CORSO ROMA – The Town Hall (Municipio) also stands on the Corso Roma. This is where the *Tavole Amalfitane* (Amalfi Tables) are kept. They are comprised of 66 chapters, in Latin and in vulgate, and were probably not the first draft of the Tables, but a later one of the 15th/16th century.
In the 15th century the tables of the codex had disappeared, but they were later found in Venice and were then taken by the Hapsburgs to the Imperial Library of Vienna. Not until 1930 were they returned to Amalfi and ever since they are on exhibition in the great hall of the Municipio.
They established all the laws for those who went to sea: the prices for hire of boats, the duties of the sailors, the responsibilities of the captains, the subdivision of profits, what to do in case of shipwreck, or abandoning ship or goods, insurance indemnities.

The "Tavole Amalfitane", on display in the City Hall.

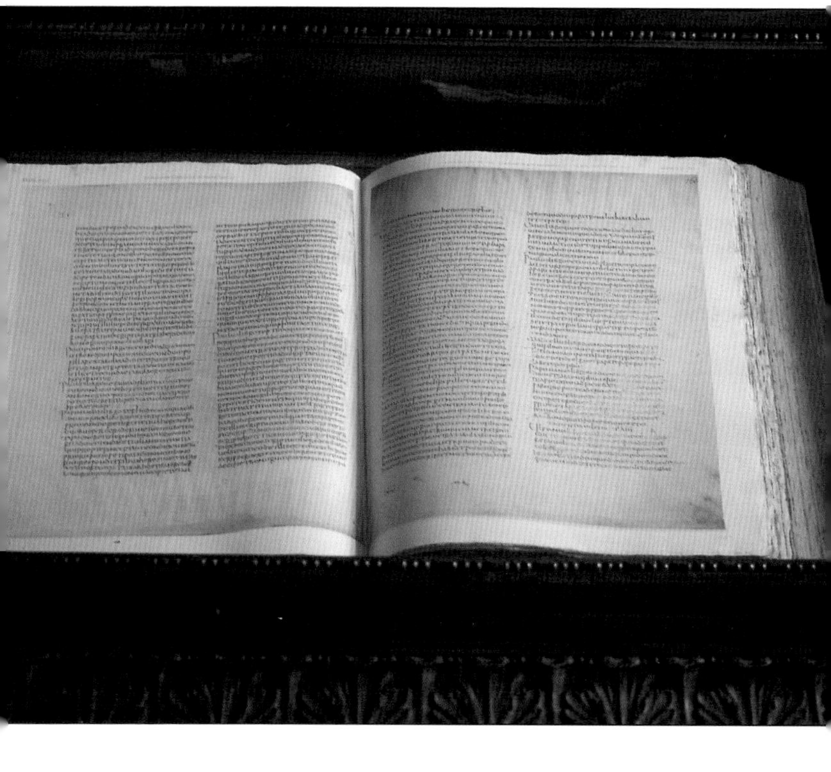

PIAZZA FLAVIO GIOIA – From Piazza Duomo one can enter the adjacent Piazza Flavio Gioia, which overlooks the sea. At the center is the *bronze monument* to Flavio Gioia, who was born in 1302 and who, as is inscribed on the base, "made navigation easier and the greatest discoveries possible" thanks to his invention, the compass.
Historically it would appear more likely that the compass was invented by the Chinese in the 7th century and that it then passed to the Arabs who introduced it to the western world. Since Amalfi was on close trading terms with the Arab peoples, it was undoubtedly one of the first to learn about the compass and its possible use at sea.

PORTA DELLA MARINA – Some of the streets in Amalfi are decorated with interesting ceramic panels: the finest is by Diodoro Cossa, and shows various phases of the construction and urban development of Amalfi: an homage of the citizens to their home town, in remembrance of more resplendent times.
There is another panel near the old Porta della Marina which reproduces an old nautical chart and takes us back in time: it is a reproduction of the southeast Mediterranean as it was known in the centuries when Amalfi was queen of the seas.
Below the panel is a boat which is still used today for the *Historical Regatta*, the great celebration of the sea and the people of Amalfi. On the day chosen there is a procession with the traditional 10th-13th century costumes and four boats take part in a race meant to recall the pomp of the ancient Maritime Republics which were always vying with each other for supremacy of the seas. The celebration, of great interest for the tourist, is in early June and each year in turn one of the four cities that were maritime republics hosts it.
During the historical procession 80 personages apiece are charged with representing the most important events in their history: a sort of giant theatric enactment with the cities themselves as stage sets.
In the race there are eight oarsmen per boat, each of which recalls the original both in form and color: Amalfi is distinguished by blue, Genoa by white, Pisa by red, and Venice by green.

Yet another testimonial to Amalfi's great seafaring tradition: the bronze monument to Flavio Gioia, the man who invented the compass.

Porta della Marina: ceramic tile maps illustrating the Mediterranean as it was known during the era of the Republic of Amalfi.

This makes it easy even for the growing crowd of foreigners who come to see these historical folklore manifestations to recognize the crews and take sides.
The prize, a scale model in gold and silver of an antique vessel, is kept with great honor in the winning city for a year, and is then once more offered as a prize the following year.
The old shipbuilding yard is at the beginning of Via Camera. The vessels made here were the fortune of Amalfi n the sea and touched on all the Mediterranean ports, permitting Amalfi to set up a dense network of trade relations.

Piazza Flavio Gioia, next to the Cathedral.

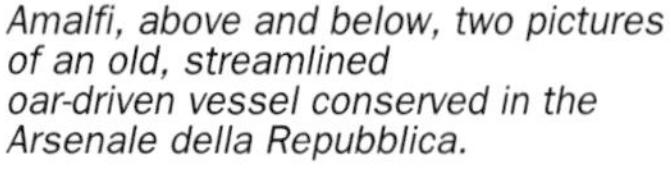

Amalfi, above and below, two pictures of an old, streamlined oar-driven vessel conserved in the Arsenale della Repubblica.

The entrance to the old Arsenale della Repubblica, which now hosts exhibits dedicated to the figurative arts.

ARSENALE DELLA REPUBBLICA – The old building consists of two large halls with large pointed arches in stone, which today rest on only ten piers, for the other twelve have been swallowed up by the sea.
The ships built there were the finest and largest of their time, equipped with as many as 116 oars, more than those of the ships built by the other Maritime Republics. Numerous models of ships are also on exhibit in the Arsenal.

/ear Amalfi, the Museo della Carta, with old tools from Amalfi's paper mills.
;elow, a splendid sunset over the gulf.

URROUNDINGS OF AMALFI – An outing to be made from Amalfi is to the *'alle dei Mulini*, or Valley of the Mills, about two hours away on foot. The tarting point is in the center, in Via Genova and Via Capuano. After leaving he city, the route follows the erosion canal of the torrent Chiarito, along a leasant road which winds along between citrus groves and brooks, with vaterfalls that once furnished power to the paper mills which flourished ere and which have now been practically abandoned.

Amalfi and its beach.

Amalfi was one of the first places in Europe to make paper with an antique procedure of Chinese derivation, which the Amalfi people had learned from the Arabs. In the 19th century the city still supplied the entire Realm of Naples with this paper, which was prized above all for public documents.
The manufacturing process consisted in taking cotton or linen rags and pounding them with pestles in tubs with water until they turned to pulp. This pulp was then poured into frames with a dense metal net so that the liquid could drain off and the vegetable fibres could dry. Once it had been smoothed and cut by hand, the sheet of paper was ready.
Evidence of this industrious activity exists today in the **Museo della Carta a Mano** (Museum of hand-made paper) as well as in the mills scattered throughout the valley of the torrent Chiarito. The museum is housed in the old paper mill, in the same valley, which belonged to the Milano family. By observing the old tools, it is possible to reconstruct the different phases of the transformation process.
By climbing up a road of about 1000 steps from the Valle dei Mulini one can also reach *Pogérola*, where there are two charming small churches, dedicated one to S. Marina and the other to the Madonna delle Grazie.
A beautiful view over Amalfi and the coast can be enjoyed from the old fortified castle.

ATRANI

Atrani still lives from the reflected light of the golden period in which it was joined to Amalfi and was the dwelling place of the most notable citizens of the Maritime Republic.
The Doge who was to guide the political destiny of the city was elected in the church of S. Salvatore. During a solemn religious ceremony the cap which conferred this power was placed on his head. And the same church, which ever since then has been called S. Salvatore de' Bireto (bireto-berret), was considered the place most worthy for their burial.
The city opens on the sea like an amphitheater, and the sight of the houses, painted in pastel colors like so many others on the Amalfi Coast, set against the vivid blue of the marvelous sea, is particularly striking.
Urbanistically the city is once more characterized by stairs, instead of by streets and alleys. Stairs join houses, the gardens, the mountain, the sea.
Atrani still looks more typically medieval than most other places. It has remained a built-up area where the neighborhoods are huddled up around their churches, which serve as points of reference to the population.
The **Cathedral** is dedicated to S. Maria Maddalena. The rich Baroque facade is part of the numerous renovations it was subjected to from 1274 on, the year when it was founded.
The dome is covered with brightly colored majolica tiles. The bizzarre bell tower is square in plan with an eightsided two-story belfry.
The interior is interesting, above all the high altar, with a wealth of polychrome marbles, above which is the canvas depicting *St. Magdalen between St. Sebastian and St. Andrew*, attributed to Giovannangelo D'Amato, a painter from nearby Maiori.

Atrani, the city is like an amphitheater over the sea at the mouth of the Valle del Dragone.

Atrani, the cathedral with its tiled dome and bizarre bell tower dominates the panorama.

Atrani: the nineteenth century facade of S. Salvatore where the elections for the doge of the maritime republic used to be held, and below, details of the village and Piazza Umberto I.

But undoubtedly the most fascinating religious building in Atrani is **S. Salvatore**, not only because of history which has left its mark but also because of the magnificent *doors* which decorate the facade. They too come from Constantinople (like the ones of the Cathedral of Amalfi) and were cast there for Pantaleone di Mauro in 1087.The building of S. Salvatore dates back to about a century before the doors, but its present forms date to 1810, the year in which the church was completely remodeled.
The interior, which was also renovated at the time, contains a precious marble plaque, a transenna of the 12th century in Byzantine style, which is sculptured in low relief with two peacocks on either side of a palm.

RAVELLO

As a result of its millennary prosperity, Ravello is unquestionably the most elegant of the small cities of the Amalfi Coast.
The foundation dates of the city are uncertain. According to an old Amalfi chronicle it was founded in the 6th century, during the second Gothic war, by a group of Romans who sought refuge here. But the first sure mention of the town is in a document of the 11th century.
Here we learn that at the time Ravello was already subjected to Amalfi, against which it attempted to rebel. It was however recaptured and included in the Amalfi duchy. This fact constituted its economic fortunes, and the two cities aided each other reciprocally. When Pisa, which was attempting to conquer the Maritime Republic, launched its first attack, it was thanks to the resistance offered by Ravello that Roger the Norman managed to arrive with reinforcements and defeat the invaders. The Pisans remembered this when they once more laid siege and won, sacking Ravello with a spirit of revenge. Later, in the middle of the 17th century, the coup de grace to the power of Ravello was inflicted by the plague which decimated the inhabitants. Even now a comparison of the number of inhabitants is striking: in the 10th century the city had a population of 30,000; now there are about 2,600.
The Arabic influence visible in the architecture and in many of the artistic expressions dates to the period when trade with the Orient was flourishing and cultural exchange intense: remains of the time are perhaps more numerous and better preserved here than elsewhere. Many of the houses have antique columns next to the entrance, and the many churches are all highly interesting.

Ravello: lush Mediterranean vegetation frames the splendid view from Villa Rufolo.

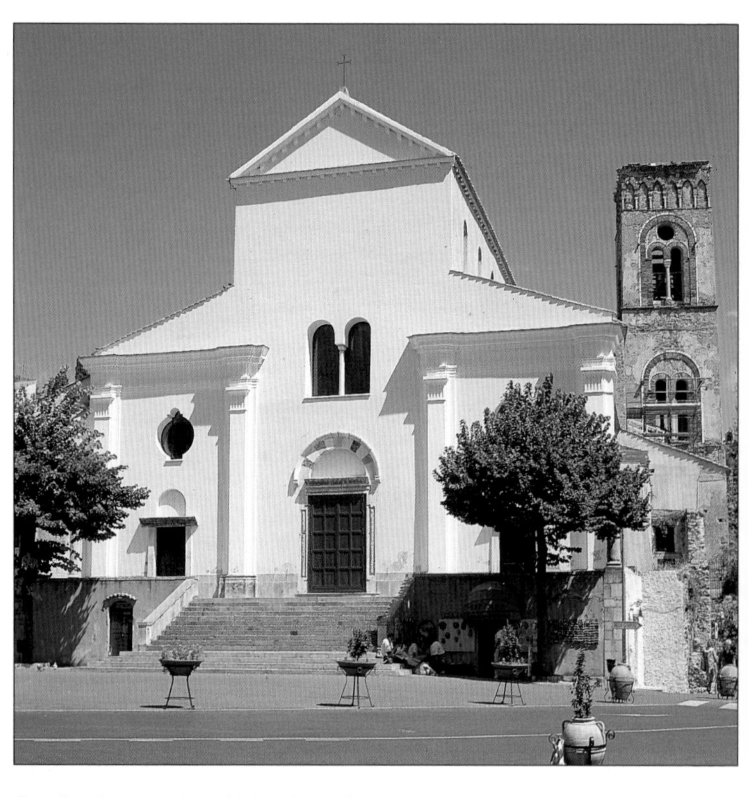

Ravello, the cathedral with its simple facade.

CATHEDRAL – The other drawing card of Ravello is the Cathedral, a treasure chest of precious works of art. The building dominates the central Piazza Vescovado, around which all the automobile traffic of Ravello is centered. In fact cars are allowed as far as the square where they may park, and the built-up area thus enjoys an undisturbed peace and tranquility.
The Cathedral, dedicated to St. Pantaleon, was founded in 1086 by the first bishop of Ravello, Orso Papirio. The building is simple in appearance: the sober facade, bare of polychrome ornament, still has the three oculi and the central two-light opening which were part of the original church. In the course of the centuries there have been various renovations, the last of which dates to 1786. Recently restoration has attempted to make the most of the original structures. The Rufolo family, the owners of the villa nearby, contributed financially. They had always participated in the artistic life of Ravello, taking on themselves the most prestigious commissions.
An imposing staircase leads up to the Cathedral. The entrance was once preceded by a pronaos, which was however destroyed by an earthquake and of which no trace remains.

THE EXTERIOR OF THE CATHEDRAL – The **bronze doors** in the center of the facade are magnificent. Cast in 1179 by Barisano da Trani, they depict the *stories of the Passion, saints and warriors* in 54 panels. They were commissioned by Sergio Muscettola, a wealthy patrician of Ravello, mentioned in an inscription in one of the panels of the right wing.

Some details of the 54 panels on the magnificent bronze door of the cathedral. This page, the panel with the inscription telling how the door was built.

S GEORGI

PAVLVS

S EVSTAS

It is important to note that bronze in the 11th-12th centuries was the material most widely used in the creation of religious works of art. Around thirty doors were marvelously cast in that period for churches throughout Europe. Twenty of these doors are in Italy, most of them in the south, scattered throughout Campania, Puglia, Sicily and Abruzzi.
For Southern Italy the commercial ties which Amalfi had established with Constantinople were important, and the munificence of the Pantaleone family which lived there left its mark on art. They had a series of doors made which were sent to Amalfi, Atrani and Salerno (to cite only those in the area in question) where they influenced the local artists. This specifically Byzantine technique consisted of flat panels in which the figures were engraved and then enriched with insertions of silver and enamel. All this was absorbed by the Italian sculptors such as Barisano. In his works in Ravello, Trani and Monreale the figures are in very low relief and the themes, such as the tree of life (in the lower band of the two leaves) or the stylized ornamental flower motives, come from Byzantine iconography.
We know practically nothing of the life of the artist. If it were not for the fact, unusual at the time, that the artist had signed his works, we would not even know his name. The 54 panels of the doors depict the *Passion* and the *Resurrection of Christ, Angels and Saints, Apostles, Prophets*. The great number of figures is explained by the fact that in the Middle Ages the portals of the churches were considered places of instruction before which penitents and neophytes paused and from which they learned by reading the sculptured iconographic program; a spiritual and visual preparation of the believers who were preparing to enter the house of the Lord.
Mention has been made to the unusual figures Barisano included on the doors of Ravello: two archers and two warriors facing each other with clubs. These motives are often encountered in Byzantine art: probably a reflection of the secular interests of the aristocracy bound to the court of Constantinople, with pastimes such as hunting and war games.

INTERIOR OF THE CATHEDRAL – The marvels of the Duomo of Ravello are naturally not limited to the doors: the interior, with a nave and two aisles, preserves precious examples of art. The remains of Roman sarcophagi are at the beginning of the right aisle.
Of particular note in the nave is a 13th-century **pulpit** by Niccolò di Bartolomeo da Foggia, commissioned by Nicola Rufolo, whose name, together with that of his wife Sigilgaita, is set into a marble panel. The decoration of the pulpit is extremely elegant: polychrome mosaics, inlays, twisted columns. Six roaring lions support the rectangular box, an eagle serves as lectern. It should be remembered that the animals allude symbolically to the power of the Church.
Niccolò di Bartolomeo was an outstanding figure in the artistic culture of Puglia-Campania in the 13th century. Of particular note among the various elements by his hand is the head of a woman with a diadem, finely executed, which is in the museum recently installed in the rooms under the Cathedral of Ravello and to which a staircase at the right of the aisle leads.
For many this woman is an idealized representation of the city of Ravello; for others it could be the portrait of Sigilgaita Rufolo or of her sister-in-law, Anna della Marra, wife of Matteo Rufolo, another member of the family who held important offices in Puglia. Originally the head was set above the small trilobate door which served as entrance to the pulpit. Below the pulpit is a 13th-century gold-ground panel of the *Madonna and Child with St. Nicholas of Bari*.
Another interesting piece of 12th-century art stands across from the pulpit, an **ambo** commissioned by

The interior of the cathedral of Ravello: one of the marble lions at the base of the pulpit and a section of a spiral column.

the bishop of Ravello, Costantino Rogadeo, with an unusual mosaic decoration showing Jonah swallowed and then spit up by the *pistrice*, an imaginary animal something like a winged dragon, symbolizing the death and resurrection of Christ.

Other treasures in the Duomo of Ravello include two interesting medieval columns used to support the paschal candle in the presbytery. To be noted also is the bishop's throne, in part composed with mosaic-decorated fragments, and columns taken from the pulpit. To the left of the high altar is the *chapel of St. Pantaleon*, patron saint of the city, whose relics are preserved in a partially gilded silver coffer, chased in 1759 by Nicola Schisano. The saint is shown holding the martyr's palm (he was beheaded at Nicomedia in 305). Nearby, in a large phial, is the blood which is said to have gushed from his throat when he was killed and which liquifies on the feast day of St. Pantaleon, July 27th, in memory of the martyr, while the worshippers cry miracle. Outstanding 13th-century marble plaques are also preserved in the *Cathedral museum*. They are decorated in mosaic with dragons, birds, stylized flower ornaments. To be noted also a fine marble sarcophagus, sculptured in low relief in the middle of the 14th century.

The interior of the cathedral of Ravello: the elegant 13th century pulpit with details of a capital and a mosaic; below, the splendid ambo opposite the pulpit.

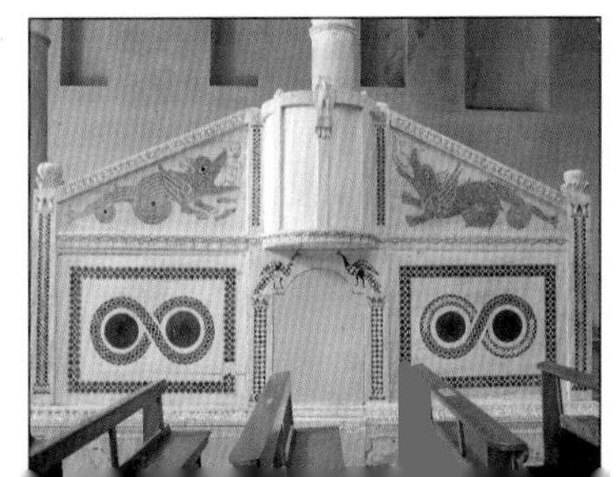

Ravello, Villa Rufolo, an overview with the gardens; it is in this picturesque setting that Wagner composed his opera "Parsifal".

VILLA RUFOLO – Along the streets many plaques are dedicated to the local families who played an important part in the development of the city; but the family most deserving of mention is the Rufolo. Still today its contribution to the prestige of Ravello is outstanding: Villa Rufolo is, in fact, one of the beauties to be seen in this charming place.
In the 13th century the Rufolo family, originally from Rome, had their mansion built here. They were extremely wealthy and owned ships and banks in Puglia and Sicily. Boccaccio makes mention of Landolfo Rufolo in the fourth novella of the second day of the Decameron. In 1275 the king even gave him his own crown as guaranty for a loan in gold.
The entrance to the villa consists of a *tower* with an ogival portal, over which are two crocodile heads. The villa in Arab-Norman style is highly interesting. The Rufolo love for beauty, to which the numerous art commissions in Ravello testify, turned the interior into a sumptuous and elegant dwelling. Many illustrious guests stayed here, including Pope Hadrian IV in 1156, and Charles and his brother Roberto. After the Rufolo, the villa passed into the hands of other noble families: the Confalone, the Muscettola and lastly the D'Afflitto. But the man who bought it in 1851, restored and opened it to the public, was a Scotchman named Nevil Reid, who loved the past glories and beauties of Ravello, where he often stayed. At present Villa Rufolo is the seat of the Institute for Research and the Restoration of the Monuments in the Ancient Centers and for the Preservation of their Urban Setting.
A splendid vista over the sea is to be had from the **gardens**, the most famous part of the villa. It is said that in 1882, when Wagner was a guest in Positano, he came here on muleback to find inspiration for his "Parsifal". Upon entering he exclaimed: "The garden of Klingsor has been found!" alluding to the scene in the second act of the opera which the emotions aroused by the gardens had suddenly brought to mind. A terrace, known as the "Wagner Terrace" recalls this episode. In summer openair concerts are held in the gardens, in the midst of this setting of trees, flowers and ocean.
Other musicians, such as Grieg and Verdi, were also struck by the gardens of Villa Rufolo, even though no direct reference appears in their works.
In the gardens are to be found a 9th-century ambo depicting a peacock and other examples of antique sculpture.

The gardens of Villa Rufolo.
Below, left, the entrance portal.

Of interest too is the small *cloister* which dates to the 13th century, with its portico of airy pointed Siculan arches, surmounted by two orders of loggias decorated with polychrome stone. The palmette decoration reveals Arabic influence.
The countless varieties of plants and flowers which delight the eye and our sense of smell are also to be admired.

*Villa Rufolo: several views of the lush gardens rich in flowers and colors;
exotic plants, cypresses and pines all flourish here.
The old tower with its fine double-lighted windows and surrounded by greenery;
a splendid panorama of the sea.*

VILLA CIMBRONE – Another of the wonders of Ravello which has to be included in a visit to the city is the Villa Cimbrone, set in a panoramic site, a bizzarre construction in medieval style, with its towers and loggias enveloped in a splendid natural setting.
The villa and the park were built at the beginning of the 20th century for the English nobleman, William Bechett.
To the left on entering is the **cloister** (dated 1917) similar in form to the one in the nearby church of S. Francesco which dates to the 13th century. In the center of the arcade are two boar heads, the family coat-of-arms of Beckett, who in the meanwhile had become Lord Grimthorpe.
The well with its majolica covering at the center of the cloister is charming and is also in the medieval style William Bechett was so fond of. The bas-relief of the seven capital sins, symbolically crowned by the Lamb with the divine Cross, is also to be found in the cloister. A staircase leads from here to the neo-Gothic crypt, supported by columns and pointed arches and dating to 1913.
There is much of interest in the **park**, both from the point of view of the naturalist, and for the fine views provided. No tourist can ever forget his visit here. The magnificent flower beds act as backdrop to a small Doric temple with a *statue of Ceres* inside, the *temple of Bacchus*, at the center of which stands the bronze statue of a satyr holding the child Bacchus, the reproduction of Verrocchio's David in the Bargello Museum in Florence. Other build-

Ravello: two views of the park and the unusual Villa Cimbrone.

Villa Cimbrone: Medieval style towers and loggias; below the cloister with its tile-covered well in the middle.

Following pages, the magnificent view of Ravello from Villa Cimbrone.

CHIOSTRO

Ravello, a detail of the "Belvedere dell'infinito" at Villa Cimbrone.

ings include a tea-room with the main facade done in imitation of the Pazzi Chapel in Florence. A grotto containing a marble Venus completes the decoration of the gardens of Villa Cimbrone.

BELVEDERE – The Belvedere, on the furthest outcrop of the rock on which Ravello stands, offers the visitor a vista the likes of which are hard to find. It has in fact been called "the belvedere of the infinite" because the eye sweeps on and on, from Atrani to the gulf of Salerno, to the plain of Paestum, to the point of Licosa.

Villa Cimbrone, the statue of Ceres in the little temple of the "Belvedere dell'infinito" and one of the busts decorating the balustrade that runs along the terrace that offers a view stretching to infinity.

CHURCH OF SAN GIOVANNI DEL TORO – In concluding one's visit to Ravello, the church of S. Giovanni del Toro should not be overlooked. Originally constructed in the 12th century, it still preserves its original aspect despite various renovations.
The sober facade is articulated by three portals. The interior merits a visit, above all for the 12th-century *pulpit*, built by a wealthy family of Ravello, the Bovio, at Alfano da Termoli. In this case too the decoration is mosaic, with allegorical subjects such as Jonah and the *pistrice*, a mythical whale.
The *crypt* of the church, decorated with 14th-century frescoes, is also lovely.

SCALA

Scala vaunts Roman origins and was already flourishing in the early centuries of the Empire. Like the other centers of the coast, it expanded economically during the centuries of the Maritime Republic, but also partook of their trials and tribulations. In 1073 the town was destroyed by Robert the Guiscard, and in 1135 and 1137 it was sacked by the Pisans, completely eliminating any possibility that remained of a comeback.

The most important monument of Scala artistically speaking is the **Cathedral**, dedicated to St. Laurence. Originally built in the 12th century, it is now Baroque in form after being remodelled.

The **interior** was also transformed in the 17th and 18th centuries, but still has two medieval crypts, one of which has two aisles with cross vaulting supported by four columns.

Many fine works are preserved inside: the *majolica pavement* of 1853 is to be noted first of all. At the back of the nave is a pulpit on four columns, brought here in 1597 from the destroyed church of Ognissanti: the mosaic decoration is striking. The *treasure of the cathedral of Scala* also includes a bishop's miter decorated in enamel which was donated by Charles of Anjou. The crypt mentioned above is entered from the right aisle. On the high altar are wooden sculptures of *Christ on the Cross*, the *Virgin and St. John,* both dating to 1260. Note also the *tomb of the Coppola family*, built in 1399 and decorated with a baldachin adorned with many figures. Among the secular buildings in Scala, mention should be made of the small groups of houses to be reached on foot in a few minutes.

Scala with Ravello and the coast in the background.

A panoramic view of Scala nestled among the sloping, terraced vineyards.

From the Cathedral, Via *S. Pietro* leads to the neighborhood of the same name, which has a tiny church with cross vaulting over the aisles and a fine *14th-century bas-relief* of St. Catherine inside.Nearby is the Palazzo Sasso, now a farm house, which belonged to the family of Fra' Gerardo Sasso, founder of the Order of the Hospitallers or of St. John. Further on is *S. Caterina*, another small group of houses around a small church, with interesting capitals on the

Scala, the facade of the cathedral of San Lorenzo.

Interior of the cathedral of San Lorenzo: a close-up of the tiled floor with the city's coat of arms.

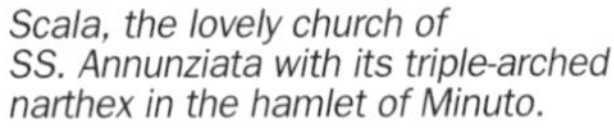

Scala, the lovely church of SS. Annunziata with its triple-arched narthex in the hamlet of Minuto.

The central door of the church of SS. Annunziata surmounted by a Byzantine fresco.

columns which separate the nave and side aisles.Still further on is *Campidoglio*, a grouping centered on the small two-aisled church of the Annunziata. Also of interest is the church of S. Giovanni Battista, in Arabian style, and the Esposito house, 13th century, with Moorish vaulting in the atrium and a columned courtyard with Moorish arches.Another group of houses is *Pontone*, particularly rich in works of art, such as the ruins of the church of S. Eustachio of the 12th century, without doubt one of the loveliest in the area, and the churches of S. Filippo Neri and of S. Maria al Carmine, both in Byzantine style. The remains of an ancient castle stand on a rocky spur.In the nearby hamlet of *Minuto*, the **church of SS. Annunziata** is worth of visiting. Erected in early Christian forms in the 12th century it sports a beatiful triple-arched narthex built with reused material.

Scala, the Torre dello Zirro in the hamlet of Pontone.

The villages of Maiori and Minori, two of the most popular spots in the area.

MAIORI AND MINORI

After Ravello the road offers a splendid panorama of the bay of **Maiori** and the mountains that surround it like an amphitheater.
The built-up area in part overlooks the ocean, behind a narrow sandy beach, in part the interior of the valley, next to the canalized course of the torrent *Reginna Maior*. This was the old name of Maiori, to distinguish it from *Reginna Minor*, which is now called Minori.
Both followed the vicissitudes of the Amalfi Republic, but after the attack by Pisa, Maiori became a feud of the D'Anjou, then of the Sanseverino and then of the Piccolomini who built the castle of S. Nicola in 1468 to defend the population from pirate incursions.
Minori received great privileges from the Norman sovereigns, but in the 11th

The picturesque stretch of road that links Maiori and Minori.

The seaside at Maiori with the Mezzacapo castle in the background.

RISTORANTE PIZZERIA

Maiori, the impressive Norman tower, the lovely cove and below, the church of S. Maria a Mare with its tiled dome dominates the village.

century it was seriously damaged by a tidal wave and a century later another cataclysm submerged most of the beach.
In the outskirts of **Minori** are the remains of a **Roman villa** dating to the 1st century A.D., an indication of the importance of the site at the time.
The center of the construction is a courtyard, once a garden, with a pool of which the plumbing system is still clearly visible. A portico with large arches and a nymphaeum decorated with stuccoes and frescoes, the remains of a staircase which led to the upper floor, and terraces, testify to the way in which the building was built with the landscape in mind. An antiquarium installed in one of the rooms of the villa contains the remains of other buildings in the surroundings.

Minori, an aerial view of the coast and pictures of the remains of the Roman villa.

Minori, the Basilica of S. Trofimena from above, and the facade with fishing boats in the foreground.

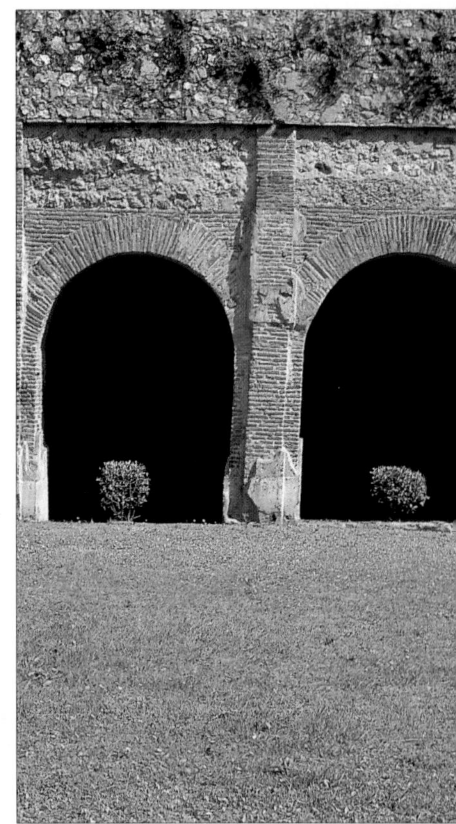

BASILICA S.TROPHIMENAE V.M

VIETRI SUL MARE

Proceeding eastwards along a harsh and rugged coast, we cross *Capo d'Orso* and come to a locality of extremely ancient origin, Vietri sul Mare, the Etruscan Marcina, which suffered the domination of the Samnites, the Lucanians and the Romans, the destruction of the Vandals and the favour of the Longobards, as well as the inevitable Saracen sackings. Situated in one of the most beautiful and suggestive areas of the coast, immersed in the greenery of a lush vegetation, Vietri today is a picturesque seaside resort boasting some impressive monuments - the *church of S. Giovanni Battista* and the *Arciconfraternita dell'Annunziata e del Rosario* - and with a thriving traditional handicraft production of ceramics which traces its origins to the Middle Ages and to which the inhabitants of the town have dedicated a museum, housed at Raito, in the tower of *Villa Guariglia*.

Vietri sul Mare: a broad panorama of the coast and the entrance to one of the typical ceramic shops. Vietri has long been famous for its ceramics.

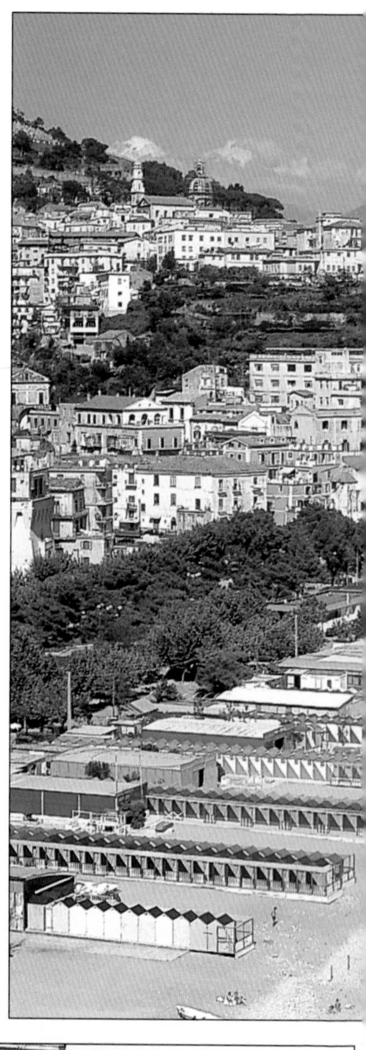

Cava dei Tirreni, the Benedictine Abbey of S. Trinità della Cava near Vietri sul Mare.

• 5

• 28

• 18

• 19

• 23

• 20/21

• 22